a guide to
HAPPINESS

a guide to
HAPPINESS

Using mindfulness and meditation

Includes
audio
meditation

TARA WARD

ARCTURUS

ARCTURUS

This edition published in 2020 by Arcturus Publishing Limited
26/27 Bickels Yard, 151–153 Bermondsey Street,
London SE1 3HA

ISBN: 978-1-83857-760-5
AD007963UK

Printed in China

CONTENTS

Introduction

Welcome! So you would like to feel happy? Or happier? Then you have come to the right book.

The exercises you are about to do will increase your overall level of happiness, but my intention is for you to have an even more profound experience. While we may feel generally happy a lot of the time as we go through life, mindful moments of real, unadulterated happiness are literally that: moments. The tools and techniques in this book are designed to help you have moments of pure happiness which is an emotion over and above feeling 'sort of happy' as you go about your daily life.

So you are going to have the opportunity to experience different levels of happiness, ranging from a mild happiness that may sustain you throughout the day to a deep explosion of happiness that might be a profound moment. The secret is to create lots of the latter, so your whole day becomes uplifted.

The even bigger secret is not to link your happiness levels to events or to pin your happiness on the behaviour of others. I appreciate that might be more of a challenge.

HELPFUL HINTS

I offer these during each stage. You might want to
try them all; you may find some appeal more than
others. Some help you to approach exercises in
different ways.

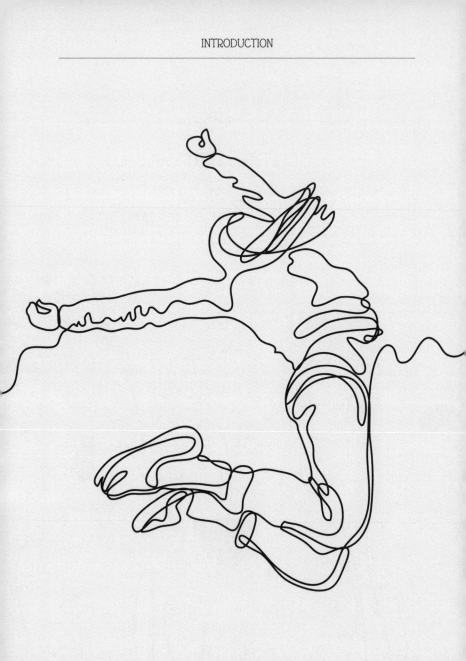

As with all my mindfulness books, I want you to have fun as we explore what true happiness means for you.

Some of the exercises might seem frivolous, but we learn much more when we are enjoying ourselves – and I want you to learn a lot!

Shall we get started? Please look at your Happiness Plan on page 118. You are going to fill it in as you go through each stage. Everyone has different triggers for happiness or unhappiness and you need to get to know yours. This is going to be a very personal journey.

I want to point out one important fact before we continue. If you suffer from clinical depression, while the techniques I offer in this book may help, I encourage you also to seek professional support.

Lastly, at the end of each section is an anecdote about my own personal journey into happiness. I hope that sharing my experiences may encourage you in your own pursuit of happiness.

PERSONAL EXAMPLE

Ever since I can remember, people have always said I come across as a happy, upbeat kind of a person. My dear Mum says I was always laughing and smiling as a young baby. But while some of us may have a greater propensity to happiness than others, I think the truth is that some of us are also better at pretending than others. I pretended a lot as a young woman; it took me a long time to realize the difference between pretending and truly being happy.

Step 1

....

Your Health

I am going to kick off by getting into a little science with you. Notice I said 'a little'!

When we are happy, our brain chemicals respond in a particular way, releasing different chemicals that have specific uses: serotonin (helps regulate our sleep), noradrenalin (gives us energy) and dopamine (determines our pleasure and pain levels).

When we are unhappy, our stress levels start to rise, causing other signals to be sent to our brain, and this is when everything begins to kick off: our adrenalin starts to increase, releasing testosterone (a hormone that regulates our feeling of dominance) and cortisol (a hormone that regulates stress levels). We go into a primal state of flight or fight, where we can no longer use reason and emotional intelligence.

This then becomes a destructive cycle. Feeling stressed and unhappy creates more chemical imbalance in our brain, which in turns affects us physically. In no time at all, we aren't sleeping properly, our energy levels drop and we start to experience aches and pains in different parts of our body. Left untreated, our brain continues to release chemicals in an unbalanced fashion, making it even harder for us to regain our equilibrium. We can lose faith in who we are and become unable to receive guidance from others. We may have brief fits of anger, followed by a debilitating depression.

You may have experienced some of that before. It doesn't feel great. Conversely, when life is good, when you feel happy, the reverse becomes possible. You sleep really well, you are full of energy and your body feels healthy and good. Your mood swings tend to become less pronounced and your emotions are more balanced.

So this brief scientific example of what can happen shows there is a very good reason to pursue happiness. It truly affects your ability to enjoy life on a physical, mental, emotional and spiritual level. In other words, choosing to be happy, instead of unhappy, can improve your life in every way.

Let's go straight into a mini-meditation so you can experience happiness on another level. This is meant to be fun. You don't need to put a lot of effort into it. Relax and enjoy it!

You have a choice, too. You can read this meditation and then follow it through afterwards, or you may wish to listen to me talking you through the meditation. If you want to hear me just click this link. (http://delivr.com/2bgbe)

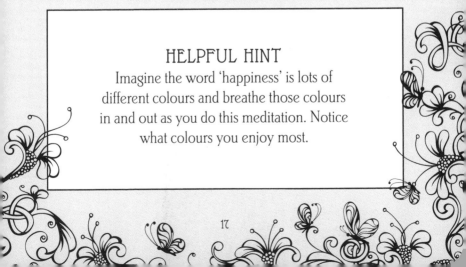

HELPFUL HINT
Imagine the word 'happiness' is lots of different colours and breathe those colours in and out as you do this meditation. Notice what colours you enjoy most.

MINI MEDITATION

You need to find somewhere quiet
to sit or lie, where you will not be
disturbed. Allow at least five minutes
to yourself for this meditation.

STEP 1:
THE 'HAPPINESS' MEDITATION

Sit or lie in your chosen space. Take a moment to make sure your body feels comfortable. Wriggle a bit if that helps. Feel your body settle. It is very relaxed. Then close your eyes. Become aware of your breath, coming in through your nose and slowly releasing through your nose or mouth. Start to observe it, without trying to alter it in any way. Breathe in and silently say 'in'; breathe out and silently say 'out'. Repeat this three times. In. Out. In. Out. In. Out.

Keeping your eyes closed, change the word and instead silently say 'happiness' as you breathe in. Repeat the word as you breathe out. Continue doing this.

Now become aware of what is happening. You may see a colour in front of your mind's eye that makes you smile. You may see an image of something or someone that makes you feel happy. Let yourself play with this experience.

Once you have absorbed an image, take an imaginary eraser and rub out the picture. Then let another image come through. Enjoy it, then erase it and see what else happens. Keep repeating the word 'happiness' silently to yourself as you breathe in and again when you breathe out.

At some point during this meditation, you may become aware of sounds, tastes or smells. Again, play with them and then let them go. Allow others to arrive and depart too.

Avoid judging what is happening; you don't need to rate your degrees of happiness. Simply enjoy the sensations while they are there. As more and more images, smells and sounds come and go, your happiness level is increasing and filling all of you.

Luxuriate in how you are feeling; this is your own personal experience of happiness. It is a very healthy state in which to be. Describe it to yourself. Be specific. Where in your body is it manifesting itself? How exactly does it feel? Try to find accurate words to explain it to yourself.

Now you are going to play a game. Remember to keep breathing comfortably as you do this. I want you to create a big, white fluffy cloud above you in the sky. It has the word 'happiness' written across it. Now, as you take a breath in, lift all of you up and on to that cloud. As you breathe out, settle into the soft folds of the white cloud. The cloud is supporting you like a fluffy duvet on top of a mattress. Relax into your cloud and realize you feel wonderfully weightless.

This is your state of happiness, unencumbered by practical, earthly issues. How do you feel now? Enjoy the sensations for a few moments. Notice what you experience. You may have images, sounds and scents here or you may just feel something different you can't quite explain. That is fine. Simply relax and allow yourself to experience it fully.

Then take a deep breath in and as you breathe out, move yourself back into your chosen place to sit or lie as you started this meditation. Feel how heavy your body is and how comfortable it feels resting against solid surfaces. Make sure you feel grounded and heavy before you open your eyes. Then take a few minutes to reorient yourself to the space in which you are sitting/lying. Stretch your limbs; perhaps give a yawn or sigh.

Slowly sit up and fill in your Happiness Plan under Step 1. Try to be as specific as you can.

When you have finished filling in Step 1, reread what you have written. Check that it accurately describes your feelings of happiness.

You might feel elated by your experience and know you want to spend more time feeling this way; you might end up feeling a little subdued, sad that you don't spend enough time in this state. Whatever your emotions, please don't worry about them or judge yourself.

Remember that this journey of embracing happiness is a very personal path. There is no 'right' way to respond to these meditations and exercises. There is only your own individual experience that is real for you.

This meditation is a great way to release those good chemicals in your brain that I mentioned earlier. Feeling happy is a physical as well as emotional experience. Enjoy being healthier. Take the opportunity to return to this

exercise whenever you can and notice how you have different experiences. Your happiness quotient may be more plentiful on some occasions than others and that is fine. You will also be returning to your cloud of happiness again and having the opportunity to enjoy it more fully. A lot more happiness awaits you.

If, from this brief meditation, you know that you want certain images or sounds around you because they make you feel happy, follow through on this as much as possible. I appreciate there are limits. If a distant holiday location made you feel wonderful, you might not have the ability to go there again immediately! But perhaps there is a photo from it that you might want to have around you.

The benefit of having a happy image available to you is that it takes you immediately into the 'now' of happiness. You don't have to think about it, or work at it, it just is.

If you notice after a while that something is not making you feel as happy as you thought, look for something new. Your triggers of happiness will change naturally over time, so it is a free-flowing process, not a static one.

When you are ready, move on to Step 2.

PERSONAL EXAMPLE

I hadn't done this meditation for a while, so I repeated it on myself. The first thing I saw was the colour yellow, followed by the image of a beautiful sunflower. I have always loved sunflowers, but I had stopped having them around me; I am not sure why. As soon as I finished my meditation, I found a photo of a sunflower field that I had taken a few years ago and made it the desktop picture on my computer. So every time I sit at my computer now, the sunflowers make me smile and I feel a rush of happiness go through me.

Step 2

· · · · · · · · · · ·

Allowing Happiness

In our previous step, I mentioned that happiness is a health-inducing state, so you might be surprised that the word 'allowing' crops up here. You may believe you don't need to allow yourself to be healthy and happy. I think you do.

People who have to work a little harder to find happiness in their lives often feel that, for whatever reason, they don't truly deserve to be happy. How much do you believe that you deserve happiness?

Play this little game overleaf to test yourself. Ask yourself the following questions and notice how many 'yes' and 'no' answers you give.

HELPFUL HINT

Sometimes we answer questions the way we think we OUGHT to answer them instead of what we really believe. Be honest with yourself.

Answer the following questions, without taking too much time to consider your reply. Note your first, gut response.

- Do you ever feel guilty if you're happy and someone around you is struggling?
- Do you sometimes feel it is wrong to be happy when there are so many troubles in the world?
- Do you ever avoid telling others you feel happy in case they are jealous?
- Do you ever tell yourself you don't deserve to be happy?
- Do you think you would be happier if only some aspect of your life were better?
- Does any of your past behaviour make you feel guilty about being happy now?
- Can you be happy only if others around you are equally happy?

If you answered 'yes' to three or more of those questions, then you probably struggle to allow yourself to feel happy on quite a few occasions.

And do you agree with some of these responses below?

- 'You shouldn't express your happiness if someone else around you is miserable.'
- 'It's insensitive even to feel happy if you know someone else is unhappy.'
- 'It's natural to feel guilty if another person is unhappy.'
- 'Everyone has past guilt; we can't help it.'
- 'You come across as smug if you're happy and the other person is miserable.'

Some of us have an ingrained belief that happiness should be enjoyed only with others who are happy and that when someone else around us is struggling, it is wrong, insensitive, rude or simply arrogant to feel happy ourselves.

I dispute this attitude. Being happy gives off a wonderful energy that can inspire others. If you let yourself sink into an unhappy state to keep someone else company, how are you benefiting either yourself or them? What do you accomplish by being miserable?

The only possible benefit is a feeling of camaraderie that comes from a shared emotion. But think of what being unhappy does to the chemicals in your brain, how it makes you feel, both emotionally and physically. Why share that when you could end up sharing something much nicer?

So this step is about acknowledging that you have every right to be happy and that you should allow yourself to be happy as often as possible, irrespective of what is happening around you.

Answer the question in Step 2 of your Confidence Plan about what you think is your biggest reason for not allowing yourself to be happy sometimes.

Now let's move on to the next meditation. Please find somewhere private where you won't be disturbed and spend at least five minutes on this.

STEP 2:
THE 'ALLOWING HAPPINESS' MEDITATION

Sit or lie in a comfortable position. Close your eyes and focus on your breathing for a few minutes, silently saying 'in' and 'out' as in the previous exercise.

Then, for a moment, focus on someone you know, or know of, whose energy you find generally downbeat and unhappy. Imagine being with them right now. Really imagine them clearly. They are in front of you. How are you feeling? What do you want to say to them? Do you feel sorry for them? Concerned? Irritated? How would you like to help them? Or would you rather just walk away?

When you have registered fully the impact of their energy upon you, withdraw from them. Use your eraser to rub out their presence or imagine them walking away and disappearing. Return to your breathing awareness for a few moments. Enjoy your solitude.

Now you are going to do the complete opposite; think of someone who makes you feel happy. Choose someone you have never met personally but whose energy makes you smile. It can be a fictional character if you wish, or even an animal. Just take a moment to find the right energy for you.

Once you have someone or something in mind, place that person or creature in front of you. They are with you in this very moment. See their face; enjoy their energy.

How do they make you feel? Absorb it and really let their happiness filter through into you. Take your time. You may even find yourself wanting to thank them for being with you.

When you are ready, even if you feel regretful, let their energy go and see them disappear. Know that you can have them back on another occasion. After they have gone, notice how happy you are feeling still: you remain uplifted.

Return to being aware of your breathing and then gently open your eyes.

You might want to take a moment to ground yourself before you fill in your experience in Step 2 of your Happiness Plan.

Of course the happy character will have had a positive impact on you. But were you surprised by how much the unhappy character affected you? How much guilt or sadness did you feel for them? Or did you find yourself becoming frustrated and irritated? Whatever your emotional response, you probably wanted to find a way to 'fix' them.

Yet the reality is we can't turn others into something they may not want to be, especially if they are not ready to embrace a change of attitude. But we can find ourselves wanting to do so and that energy can make us feel stressed, and lead us into a downward spiral of unhappiness.

However, when we focus on ourselves, we have the opportunity to become more useful. While we cannot take responsibility for someone else's happiness, we may be able to influence them in a positive way. During that process, is it more powerful for us to be feeling happy or unhappy? You see my point.

The power of mindfulness lies in 'being in the moment' and you choose how you want to feel in each moment.

Before we move on, return to what you believe is your biggest block to enjoying happiness. You will have made a note about this already on your Happiness Plan; it will be personal to you. Here is a simple meditation to help you eradicate that feeling once and for all.

HELPFUL HINT

Depending on how long you have held your belief, you may find this an emotional exercise. If at any point it feels too much, allow yourself to withdraw from it by imagining yourself under a beautiful waterfall or shower. Let the water wash away the emotion and realize you feel cleansed and calm when you finish.

STEP 2:
THE 'CLEARING THE
BLOCKAGE' MEDITATION

Please sit in a comfortable location
where you won't be disturbed. Have your
feet flat on the floor and let your hands
relax loosely in your lap. Close your eyes
and listen to your breathing for a few
moments. Don't try to alter it in any way
— simply observe it.

Now turn your focus on to what you believe to be your biggest block to enjoying happiness. State the issue out loud if you can. Say it silently if you have to, but still say it firmly. Then repeat the issue again, even more firmly. You are really willing to face this now and to find a solution. Then ask yourself the question, 'Why do I feel this way?' Again, ask it firmly. You want to know the answer. It could come quickly, or it may take a moment. The response may be what you expect, but don't worry if what you receive is a surprise. Accept what you get.

Repeat the answer you have been given. Notice if it makes you feel emotional. Stay with the emotion.

Then say to yourself, equally firmly, 'I don't need this emotion any more. I choose to release it.' You are now going to get rid of both your issue and the reason for you feeling the way you do, in one simple act.

However the emotion is manifesting for you, take it from your body or mind and see it being stuffed into a large helium balloon. Push your issue itself into it as well. Shove everything in. Pause to make sure it is all in there, then tie the balloon tightly and release it into the air. Watch it float away until it becomes the tiniest of specks and finally disappears altogether.

As it disappears, you will realize you feel much lighter and happier. Acknowledge yourself for letting go of something you truly didn't need. Take time to focus on your body and how heavy it feels before you open your eyes and get up.

Well done for going through this process! It is a simple meditation but a very powerful one. You may find you need to repeat it at intervals in the future and that is fine. You can fill as many helium balloons as you like over time and watch them recede into nothingness.

It is important for you to embrace the reality that there is no downside to embracing happiness, either for yourself or for others. You just need to believe you are worth all this happiness. Because you are.

Let's move on to Step 3.

PERSONAL EXAMPLE

I have spent a lot of my life trying to cheer up others. It is part of my nature. If I'm being honest, I have wasted a lot of time in this pursuit. It has taken me years to work out that the best way I can help others is simply by being myself. And the happier my frame of mind, the better I listen and can understand others. Often people who are unhappy don't want solutions thrown at them; they may even know for themselves what they should be doing, but they aren't ready to do it yet. Your happiness is not dependent upon someone else being happy too.

Step 3

·············

The Pleasurable Pursuit of Happiness

Having experienced Step 2, I hope you are in a clearer frame of mind to pursue the pleasure of happiness. It is such a joy to welcome it more fully into your life.

In the Introduction, I referred to different levels of happiness. You are going to start with the most fundamental and gradually work your way into the deeper levels.

The first level of happiness starts with what you can create around you right now that will make you feel better. I promised you fun, so this exercise will encourage you to play with ideas and explore what makes you happy. It would be helpful to have at least ten minutes for this initially; after that, this is something to which you can return whenever you wish.

Have pens, pencils and paper beside you before you start. It would be good to have different colours if you can and the larger the piece of paper, the better. You might want to stick several sheets together. You could use a large piece of cardboard. This is your game and you are the only player, so enjoy your freedom.

HELPFUL HINT

There has been a lot of research that indicates that using your other hand to write or draw can bring out another part of you. Why not embrace a new experience and switch hands? It might make the game slower, but you might also enjoy it more.

STEP 3:
THE 'PLEASURABLE PURSUIT OF HAPPINESS' GAME

Take a moment to sit in a quiet place, with your drawing tools and paper easily accessible. Close your eyes and relax. Focus on your breathing. Remind yourself that happiness is a healthy state you deserve to experience as much as possible.

Think of things that make you happy. As something comes to mind, open your eyes, pick up your pen or pencil and either write or draw it. You will probably find yourself smiling as you do this. Then close your eyes and focus on your breathing and the word 'happiness' again. Repeat the process.

After a while, you may not want to close your eyes again. Instead, you may find yourself preferring to write and draw continually as different thoughts come into your mind.

Try not to judge your reasons or analyse why something makes you feel happy. Simply enjoy the fact that it makes you feel good. Some random topics for you to consider as you do this 'game' are:

- Colours
- Images
- Locations
- Scents
- People
- Music
- Clothes
- Animals
- Mythical creatures
- Hobbies
- Food Experiences.

You may think of others. There are no restrictions, as this is your personal exploration. No one will criticize or pass comment. Enjoy yourself.

When you feel you have explored all the avenues available to you, stop and survey what you have created. Are you surprised by how much you have put down?

The next part of this game is to make 'works of art' from what you have discovered makes you happy. If you like what you have written or drawn already, that's great. I'm still going to suggest that you return to this game and that you add to it as you make your way through the steps in this book. You can do this in a variety of ways, such as:

- Find pictures in magazines or online that personify happiness to you
- Go through photos and choose ones that make you smile
- Pull out birthday cards/emails/letters that make you happy
- Have the happy music you've chosen around you, ready to play
- Keep the happy films readily accessible
- Wear your happy clothes as much as you can; keep them together in your wardrobe
- Invest in the scents that make you smile and use them a lot.

If you have struggled sometimes with feeling happy, learning to feel it now is like an exercise that you have to keep doing to get into shape. You may have forgotten how good happiness feels or been stuck in believing you didn't deserve it.

In order to move out of that phase, you need to have plenty of 'happy' things near you to reinforce what it feels like.

All the reminders help to exercise your brain and to underpin the fact that happiness is something very real that you can have now, all around you.

I would also encourage you to have happy reminders in all aspects of your life. So apart from having them in your home, find ways to put happy reminders in your working environment too. How can you have happy things in your car or on your bicycle or with you as you travel on public transport? What could you wear permanently that makes you smile? How could you incorporate it into whatever technology you use?

The more you focus on having happy things around you, the more you may realize that you have been missing out. It can be all too easy to get into routines that don't give you much joy. So although exercising the happy thoughts may feel a little 'creaky' as you start, the more you exercise, the easier it becomes until one day you realize your happiness health has improved immeasurably.

One last thing I recommend heartily is to find time for pleasurable physical exercise. It is well known that physical activity releases endorphins — hormones that help our sense of wellbeing. It doesn't matter what you choose or where you do the exercise, as long as you enjoy it. You don't have to go to the gym or take up a sport unless you want to do that: go dancing, make love or walk up a steep hill in the countryside! Be inventive. Whatever you do, simply be in the moment and enjoy it.

I wish you lots of happy exploring during this step. Take your time deciding what works best for you. When you are ready, you are going to move forward and explore a different level of happiness.

PERSONAL EXAMPLE

You will find that the triggers for this level of happiness alter as you go along. For instance, when you lose someone you love, you may find that having mementoes of them on view makes you feel sad instead of happy. When my father died, I didn't have any of his photos displayed for quite a while; after a few years, I discovered that seeing his face made me smile again. I had reached a stage in bereavement where I was ready to remember the good moments and focus on those. Don't hesitate to change what you have around you as your own feelings shift.

I used to find any form of keeping fit a struggle; it never made me happy. I spent years reluctantly going off to gyms or trying sports at which I was useless. Then I decided to approach physical activity another way: I asked a trainer to devise a series of exercises I could do at home or in any hotel room. I embellished it by deciding my warm-up would consist of dancing vigorously to my favourite music. I'm no dancer but it doesn't matter because no one watches me! In fact, when I am writing, I pause often to get up and have a little bop around my study. When I sit down again, I realize I am smiling and my energy has been lifted. It makes writing so much easier and much more enjoyable.

Step 4

· · · · · · · · · · ·

Installing Happiness Into Your Genes

Your mind is a powerful tool in determining what happens to you. It can change your brain's behaviour and in turn affect your physical body. So now you are going to use your mind to install happiness into your genes.

This process will deepen your happiness quotient and allow you to enter another level of happiness. Are you ready for this?

I mentioned in the Introduction that profound happiness is about feeling happy irrespective of what is happening to us or around us. It is a way of removing ourselves from physical challenges and seeing happiness as a state that exists separately from our earthly concerns.

I appreciate that may sound a little strange, but bear with me as we go through this step; you may find it makes a lot more sense by the end of it.

Do you remember the cloud of happiness you visited briefly in Step 1? It is time to return to it and to explore what it has to offer in more detail. So rather than my using a lot of words trying to explain what profound happiness feels like, do this meditation and see if you experience it for yourself.

HELPFUL HINT

This may be one of the best 'feel good' meditations you ever do, so please try to find enough time to enjoy it properly. Taking ten minutes to do this will be a thousand times more powerful than just taking five minutes!

STEP 4:
THE 'INSTALLING HAPPINESS INTO YOUR GENES' MEDITATION

Retreat to a quiet place where you will not be disturbed and sit upright in a comfortable chair, with the soles of your feet flat on the floor. Close your eyes. Feel your body relaxing as you breathe deeply and easily. If saying the silent 'in' and 'out' helps you to focus, please use that technique.

When you feel pleasantly relaxed, turn your attention to your white, fluffy cloud above you. Emblazoned upon it is the word 'HAPPINESS'. Notice how large the lettering is and how the cloud seems to radiate light.

Take a deep breath and then propel yourself upwards and on to the cloud.

As you breathe out, settle into the fluffy folds of the cloud and let yourself relax. Become aware of how weightless you feel.

This is because you are unencumbered by life's challenges up here. Earthly reality can't affect you because you are pure energy while you are on your cloud. Your physical body is unimportant. Enjoy this freedom. Take a while to fully experience your weightless state, both in body and mind. What does it feel like not to be bogged down by daily issues and concerns?

Know that no one will ever join you on your cloud; you will always be alone. It is your very private and personal place. Its soft, white emptiness is the perfect energy to allow you to reconnect with yourself on a soul level.

Take a few moments to embrace this properly. Describe your pure energy. How does it make you feel? Notice there are no emotions such as anxiety or sadness. There is no responsibility to be a certain way. Your soul is calm and full of peace.

Now it's time to remember you are on this cloud called happiness for a reason. Your soul needs to absorb happiness deep into your genes, to prepare you for a return to earthly life.

And this is exactly what your cloud will allow you to do: recharge yourself with happiness. This is because every atom of your cloud and the air around your cloud is infused with pure happiness. It is not earthly; it is not dependent upon good things happening. It is a limitless supply of profound happiness that exists in this sphere that is timeless and always accessible. You simply have to allow yourself to absorb it all. So choose to do it now. First, access happiness through your breathing. Take a deep breath. As you breathe in, you are taking in pure happiness. It is infiltrating all of you: body, mind and soul. Feel it penetrating deep into your very cell structure, infusing all the genes in your body with happiness. As you breathe out, feel it growing inside you. Repeat the process. Notice how effortless it is to absorb happiness while on your cloud. Keep repeating until all of you is infused with happiness.

Now you are going to take this experience even deeper. Feel your own energy, your pure soul, melt into the happiness cloud itself. Feel you and the cloud become one. There is no need to define happiness because you ARE happiness.

It has no weight. No meaning. It simply is. Stay in this state for a while.

Then, when you are ready, refocus your thoughts and visualize yourself sitting on top of your cloud again. All of you remains filled with pure happiness. At the same time, you acknowledge it is time to return to the earthly world and what awaits you.

So take a deep breath in and as you breathe out, allow yourself to swoop back to your chair, where you started this meditation. As you do, you may feel a little jolt in your physical body. It may feel like a mild shock or a bump. This is perfectly normal. Keeping your eyes closed, stay focused on your breathing. As you inhale, become aware that your body feels heavy. As you exhale, feel the weight of your body settle comfortably. Keep doing this for a few moments. Next, wiggle your toes and fingers. Then pat yourself gently: your arms and your legs. Are your legs feeling heavy and grounded? Pat them again if they still feel light. How solid do your feet feel on the ground? Focus on how each part of the soles of your feet connects with the ground.

Only then, open your eyes. Does the room feel very bright and buzzy? Focus on an object to reorient yourself. Don't get up until you feel properly grounded.

Fill in Step 4 of your Happiness Plan before you continue with your day.

So now you have a new experience of happiness. It is what I call profound happiness. How did it feel? Were you surprised by the depth of your experience? Sometimes it can be hard to put into words; it can feel as if there aren't powerful enough adjectives to describe it. Some people would call it 'bliss'; you might prefer another word.

Once you have felt it, there is no going back because for evermore you will realize that you have a choice about how much happiness you decide to feel. You can access this state whenever you wish and it costs nothing, except a little time.

It is not dependent upon what is happening to you, because you can remove yourself from life's challenges and allow yourself this happiness recharge at any time.

The more you repeat this meditation, the more you will connect with your soul's happiness. Every visit to your cloud will increase your sensation of profound happiness. Whatever you felt on your first trip, it is nothing compared to subsequent ones.

Of course the real trick is to maintain this profound happiness while at the same time dealing with the vagaries of everyday 'real' life. Let's move on to Step 5.

HELPFUL HINT

It might be useful to consider this fact. There are approximately 30,000 genes in each human cell and the average human has 37 trillion cells. Every time you visit your happiness cloud, you give yourself the opportunity to infuse yet more of your trillions of genes with profound happiness.

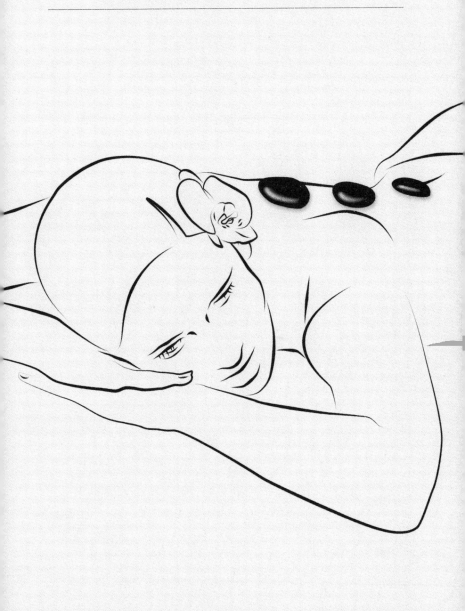

PERSONAL EXAMPLE

Discovering that my happiness was not dependent upon anyone or anything else was a major turning point in my life. It had an effect in so many ways. I didn't need to drink to get a 'buzz'; I could have difficult experiences and know I wouldn't crumble, because my happiness was not directly connected to only good things occurring. It meant that whatever was happening to me or around me, I knew I could access a moment of happiness at some point. It was truly liberating. It wasn't until life took a very challenging turn that I had to access a deeper understanding.

Step 5

···········

The Time For Happiness

It's easy to say 'I will be happier one day when ...' or 'If so and so would just happen, I could feel happier.' And if you answered 'yes' to question 5 of the Allowing Happiness game – 'Do you think you would be happier if only some aspect of your life were better?' – then this step may be especially relevant for you.

If we wait for life to be better so we can feel happy, most of us are going to wait a long time. Even then, we may reach a stage when everything feels great, only to have something unexpected come along and shatter our perfect existence. Life has a habit of throwing us curve balls from time to time, usually when we least expect it.

You know now that you can retreat to your happiness cloud to replenish yourself and that is a great tool at your disposal. But what would life be like if you found happiness in all the earthly circumstances too? This step is going to look at how you can access happiness no matter what is happening to you now. This takes us to the heart of mindful happiness.

How many of these statements resonate with you?

- I don't have enough money.
- I wish I were more attractive.
- Other people have better lives than me.
- I don't have much good luck.
- I'd like to be older/younger.

What would it be like to replace those thoughts with these?

- I am happy with my financial situation.
- I am happy with my looks.
- I have a happy life.
- My happiness makes me lucky.
- I am happy being the age I am now.

What feels more natural to you? If it is the second set, that's great. Your happiness quotients are coming along in great leaps and bounds. If you still gravitate towards the first set, perhaps you could benefit from a few more tools in your happiness toolkit. Let's add another one.

The bottom line is that the only moment about which we can be sure is this very moment now. We can't control the past and no matter how much we might like to map out the future, we just never know what is going to happen next to us.

So finding a way to say, 'I am happy right now,' and to mean it is true mindful happiness. It leads to a great sense of contentment. You have some tools already to help you. You know you can have things around you that encourage happiness, you can use physical exercise to increase your endorphins, you have your balloon technique to banish blocks to happiness and you can retreat to your happiness cloud for a top-up.

You also have the option to programme your mind to accept the happiness mode when you wish. Now that you know you can feel happiness in different ways, you want to find a way to assure your mind that this is true. Sometimes our mind can take a while to be persuaded, so the next meditation is to help this process. The premise is a simple mantra: a repeated use of words.

HELPFUL HINT

Remember that mindfulness is about being in the moment. The power in this meditation comes from really experiencing each moment of it, step by step.

STEP 5:
THE 'I AM HAPPY NOW' MINI-MEDITATION

Retreat to a quiet place and sit or lie comfortably. Close your eyes and focus on your breathing for a few moments. Use the 'in – out' technique to ensure you become deeply relaxed.

Now say to yourself, 'I choose happiness.' Notice what happens to you when you say it. You may have a pleasurable rush; you may find doubts rushing in.

Whatever your response, repeat the words, 'I choose happiness.' Any time you get a negative response ('Oh, no you don't' or 'You don't deserve it'), repeat your statement.

You know that happiness is a choice that you can embrace whenever you want it. Choose it now. Keep saying, 'I choose happiness.'

When the doubting thoughts have subsided, change what you say slightly to 'I am happy.' Notice if you feel a difference. If doubts creep in again, repeat, 'I am happy.'

Now allow yourself to feel it. You know what it is like; you have experienced it during previous exercises. Let yourself feel it right now. Your soul being immersed in happiness on your happiness cloud: that is you.

You do not need a reason or any person to make you feel happy. You can feel happy at any time, under any circumstances.

You control your happiness. Bring it on now. Right this minute. Feel happy. Go on. Enjoy it. Feel yourself smile. Feel happiness well up inside you. There is no particular reason for your happiness. You don't need one. You just ARE happy. Repeat, 'I am happy.' Mean it.

Let yourself stay in this state for a while. Then, when you feel ready, open your eyes.

Keeping your eyes open, glance around you, and keep repeating, 'I am happy'.

Notice how everything looks now. Notice how you feel.

When you are ready, fill in Step 5 of your Happiness Plan.

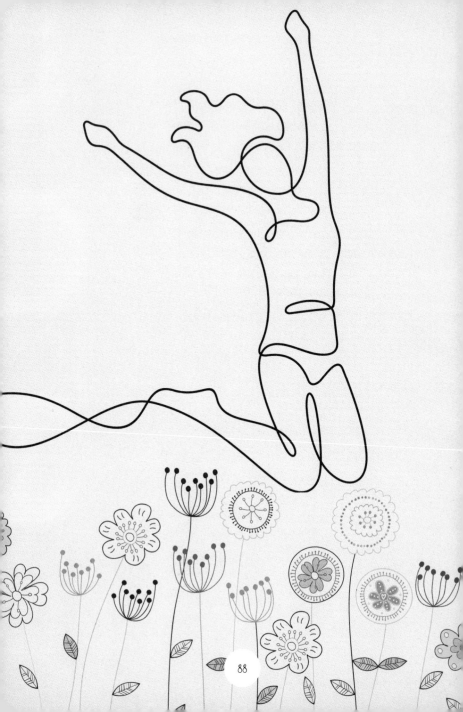

How happy do you feel now? This experience will be different for everyone. You may have found it surprisingly easy to decide to be happy for no specific reason; you may have discovered a lot of doubts.

The power of using a few simple words and repeating them is that your brain processes words and their meaning. The more we choose to input certain words on a regular basis, the more quickly our brain responds.

This step is a very basic one, but it has infinite possibilities. Practise saying, 'I am happy,' throughout your day. As you wake up, let your first words be 'I am happy.' As you go about your daily tasks, especially if you find one daunting, before you start, say, 'I choose happiness.' Now that you know you can feel happiness and have access to it, your choice for the future is to access it whenever you wish.

Let's move to Step 6.

PERSONAL EXAMPLE

In my experience, this step doesn't work unless you have spent time immersing yourself in the feeling of profound happiness from Step 4. In other words, this stage is a reinforcement of something you already know; it doesn't work if you are still uncertain and trying to convince yourself that you can be happy. I said, 'I am happy,' to myself a lot when I was younger, though I was nothing of the sort. It didn't work because I hadn't delved any deeper into myself at that stage. I didn't understand where my lack of happiness came from, nor had I experienced a state of profound happiness. I just kept dealing with surface issues and hoping that would suffice. If you find your 'I am happy' mantra leaves you feeling a little 'hollow', it may be that your own experience of profound happiness has yet to be fully formed.

Sometimes, a major event in your life can make it easier to access this deeper level of experience. Paradoxically, my ability to understand true happiness really crystallized during the most difficult time in my life: when my husband was diagnosed with advanced bowel cancer.

Step 6

....

Everything Makes Me Happy

So the next stage is to find happiness in every part of your life, on a daily basis. Your ability to feel happy is a very personal and powerful choice. You decide if you want to feel happy – no one else can do this for you.

The reality that no one else can make you happy is a difficult one for some people.

After all, surely one of life's greatest joys is to love and be loved. Is our happiness not dependent upon that emotion: both the giving and receiving of it?

I dispute that. The deepest level of profound happiness comes from within you, from your soul, and it is not dependent upon someone else loving you. That is why your happiness cloud is only for you; it is a retreat where you are always alone.

Of course giving and receiving love is a wonderful, vital part of our earthly life and it can certainly add to our happiness, making our daily existence more pleasurable and meaningful. But no one else has the ability to determine your true worth or to decide upon your happiness. That is your job in life.

There is a massive benefit to understanding this because when you realize you are not dependent upon others for happiness, it gives you a tremendous freedom. You can give and take, without expecting someone else to make you feel good about yourself. I believe it also makes you more attractive to others, because they see you as a person in your own right, whole and fully formed. There is another benefit, too. You know that rush of happiness we feel when someone praises us or makes us feel good for a period of time? Have you ever noticed what may follow is a feeling of deflation? We can then find ourselves in a cycle: wanting to please, receiving praise, feeling insecure again when it stops, and needing to please again. It is a repeated series of highs and lows that ultimately leaves us feeling empty – whereas when we access happiness through ourselves, all of life feels more balanced, more grounded, and our capacity to give and receive becomes a natural flow of energy, not something forced and anxious.

So, from now on, your task in daily life is to embrace what makes you happy by consciously choosing happiness and choosing to see happiness in all situations, however difficult.

Let me give you two simple examples.

1) You wake up after a disturbed night's sleep, feeling out of sorts. Your mood is dark as you remember everything you haven't done and need to do — perhaps things you dislike. You contemplate your dissatisfaction with life in general and get out of bed, decidedly grumpy. What sort of a day will unfold for you?

2) You wake up after a disturbed night's sleep, feeling out of sorts. You take a few moments to focus on your breathing. You propel yourself on to your happiness cloud and replenish yourself. You remember to feel grateful for what you have in life and start to count all the things you have that make you happy. As you get out of bed, your eyes alight on something that makes you feel happy. Then, as you start your day and several times during it, you repeat, 'I am happy,' to yourself. What sort of a day will unfold for you?

I think you see my point. We create our own happiness by determining our attitude.

Some of you may be thinking that it's fine to do that when we start the day, but what happens when we are hit by challenges throughout the day? Let's be realistic, some days can throw out a whole series of punches in our direction! Again, it is our response to those events that will determine how we move forward. When something challenges us, choosing our response is a big indicator of how happy or unhappy we will be. Let's use another example, only this time you are going to fill in two opposite responses.

Under Step 6 of your Happiness Plan you will find a theoretical challenge. Fill in what you feel is the 'happy' and 'unhappy' response route. Be as specific as possible with how you could react.

When you have finished, notice what you filled in first. Which response was the easier? Why do you think that was? Which response has more suggestions? Being honest, ask yourself which responses are you most likely to have first?

If you know you are veering more towards the happy option, please congratulate yourself.

If you feel more drawn to the unhappy, then acknowledge yourself for being honest and know you have helpful exercises to repeat that will increase your happiness in times to come.

Then finish this step with the practical exercise below that may be useful to you for the future. Please throw yourself into this exercise, have some fun with it and think up some 'silly' reasons too!

HELPFUL HINT

Have some extra sheets of blank paper to hand for this exercise; you may become inspired. Enjoy getting carried away.

STEP 6:
THE 'EVERYTHING MAKES ME HAPPY' EXERCISE

There is a section in Step 6 for you to fill in as you do this exercise. Take a moment to make sure you are sitting comfortably. Enjoy a few deep breaths. If you aren't feeling as happy as you'd like at the start, bounce yourself up on to your happiness cloud and replenish yourself before you continue.

Begin by considering how you start a typical day. What do you do first? What makes you happy about that? It doesn't have to be profound. If you start with a shower, it could be the colour of your towel or the scent of your shower gel!

Now move on to the next part of your average day. What aspect of that makes you happy? What else about it is good? Continue until you have covered major moments in your day. You will find it becomes easier and even more fun as you go along.

When you have finished, reread everything. You may be surprised by how much happiness every day can contain – provided you allow yourself to feel it, of course.

Was it a surprise to discover just how much 'good stuff' there is in your day, when you let yourself uncover it all?

I love this exercise because it often reveals so much about what we have already that we tend to take for granted, instead of appreciating.

If, during the exercise, you thought of things that you could do to increase your happiness levels, make a note and implement them wherever possible. You are now creating masses of mini-mindful moments of happiness through your day.

HELPFUL HINT

Once you have done this exercise, you might want to stick some Post-it notes around, reminding you about your happy attitudes!

You can take this one step further; if you know you have certain challenging situations coming up, determine what you can do about them that will make you happy. We can't predict unexpected events, of course, but the more we rearrange our attitude to what occurs, the easier it becomes to deal with the surprises.

When you continue doing this, and incorporate your 'everything makes me happy' attitude into all that you do, no upset is insurmountable, as I discovered (see overleaf). You can truly find happiness in everything that happens.

PERSONAL EXAMPLE

Finding lots of happiness as you nurse your partner through a terminal illness can be quite a challenge. When my husband was diagnosed with bowel cancer back in 2011, he embarked on a series of varying chemotherapy regimes over three years before sadly passing in 2014. It wasn't an easy time. I wasn't sure I would be able to find laughter and happiness through it all but in fact I did. We both did. Ray's favourite expression became 'The best of times is now' which is a perfect metaphor, of course, for mindful happiness. Naturally, we had times when humour and happiness eluded us, but we also kept open to finding happiness, especially from small moments: an unexpectedly beautiful sunset, the sweetness of a freshly baked biscuit, the smell of lilies in the room. Life became a true 'living in the moment' exercise because that moment was all we had for certain. Knowing time was limited, our love deepened and intensified. I popped up on to my happiness cloud more frequently as time went on.

But the most profound understanding of happiness came for me on the first morning after my husband had passed. I was expecting to feel dreadful. However, as I awoke, my first emotion was one of happiness. The happiness stemmed from knowing he was no longer struggling and that he was finally at peace; I felt full of gratitude for what we had shared for 23 years. His decline had been slow and difficult, so it is natural that I would feel a degree of relief. However, what I felt was far more than relief; it was profound happiness. Of course I went on to have difficult moments after that because bereavement is a sad process, but I have never, ever forgotten that moment of happiness and when I feel down, I can take myself back to that moment in bed and feel very grateful for that happiness. In fact, remembering it always uplifts me because it is my proof that happiness can come at any moment, including moments of trauma, if we allow ourselves to feel it.

Step 7

·············

Stepping Stones

So you have reached the final step. Well done! You have taken quite a journey from looking at what stops you from being happy to releasing those emotions and lastly to allowing yourself to feel happy through different means. Acknowledge yourself for what you have done.

Of course your happiness journey is not over. We are all work in progress and you may have times when your happiness levels dip for whatever reason. However, you now have tools to ensure you can find it again when you wish.

As I shared in my personal examples, you can face the most difficult time in your life and still experience happiness. Challenges don't take away happiness; they give you the opportunity to find even deeper levels.

Moving forward, there is one way to ensure you keep feeling moments of happiness: simply accept exactly where you are right now in your life. That is true mindful happiness.

Please enjoy the final mini-meditation which follows.

STEP 7:
THE 'STEPPING STONES'
MEDITATION

Find a peaceful spot in which to relax without being disturbed. Close your eyes. Spend a few minutes doing your 'in – out' breathing technique and feel your body becoming pleasantly heavy. Now, in your mind's eye, see a line in front of you, running from left to right. This is your lifeline. The far left represents when you were born and the far right is your future stretching ahead of you. Place yourself somewhere on that line now.

Look to your left: how much happiness was there in your past? Consider the answer without judging yourself or seeking any justification. Now look to your right. How much happiness do you want in your future?

Look at where you are now on your timeline. You cannot alter your past because it has gone. You can affect only this moment right now. Your future consists merely of 'in the now' moments to come. It is unknown and you can only live it, moment by moment, as you take each step.

How do you want to feel during each step from now on?

Choosing happiness means a healthier, easier life. It means whatever happens to you, you can handle it, because you are not pinning your feeling of happiness on to the events themselves.

Your happiness is who you are, not what others make you feel.

Look at the line stretching to the right of you. See that it is actually made up of stepping stones. Notice that each stone has the word 'happiness' emblazoned on it, stretching into infinity. In fact, you are standing on one right now that says 'happiness'.

This is your life. This is your choice. Each time you take another step, you are creating another 'in the now' moment of happiness. It is easy.

Look at the happiness stretching out before you. You can have it every step of your way. You simply choose to step on to the happiness stone each time. Enjoy this moment of understanding.

Then, when you are ready, focus on your body back in the space in which you chose to relax. Feel heavy and grounded before you open your eyes. Notice that the feeling of happiness remains with you.

So here is your final tool in your happiness toolkit: finding your happiness stepping stones everywhere you go. They are always there, of course. You just need to be in a mindful state to see them.

Lastly, choose to see happiness as something that is stored permanently inside you. When you visit your happiness cloud, you stock up on extra large quantities and when you return to your everyday existence, it is still inside you, waiting to be released as and when you choose. How comforting to know it is always there, whenever you want it.

From this moment on, you are the one in control of your happiness, through every single step of your journey. Enjoy it!

PERSONAL EXAMPLE

I see happiness stepping stones everywhere I go. I'm a visual person, so pictorial images work well for me. If I have a moment of dissatisfaction, I tend to look down and visualize the word 'happiness' emblazoned below me. That usually makes me smile. It may also make people wonder if I am particularly fond of my feet! Do watch where you yourself step – happiness is everywhere.

EPILOGUE

It's been a pleasure sharing my happiness thoughts with you and if *A Guide to Happiness* has helped you, please share it with others. You may want to consider a further title in this series, too: *Build Your Confidence.*

Happiness Plan

You can note down your experience of A Guide to Happiness in this workbook.

Step 1

From your **Happiness Meditation**, describe the following:
What happened when you said the word happiness?

Images

Sounds

Smells

Tastes

Feelings

What did it feel like being on your **Happiness Cloud**?
How was it different from the rest of the meditation?

What do you want to have around you now to make you feel
happy, as a result of this meditation?

Write down your number of 'yes' and 'no' answers from the
Allowing Happiness Game:

What is your biggest block to enjoying happiness?

How did the **Allowing Happiness Meditation** make you feel?
Be specific.

Who was your **Happy Person**? Why did you choose them?
What quality about them most appeals to you?

Write down the results from your **Clearing The Blockage Meditation**:

What did you choose as your biggest block?

Why do you have this block?

What method worked best to clear it?

Step 3

Describe the results of your
Pleasurable Pursuit of Happiness Game:

What stands out for you the most? Why?

How many happy reminders have you got around you?
How could you create more?

How does physical exercise increase your happiness?

Step 4

Describe how you feel after
The Installing Happiness Genes Meditation:

Step 5

How many of those statements felt true to you from the two lists?
Write down the ones with which you identify the most.

Make notes about the **I Am Happy Now Mini-Meditation**:

What was your first response when you said:
'I choose happiness'?

What followed?

What happened when you said 'I am happy'?

How many times a day do you want to say "I am happy"?
When do you want to do this?

Theoretical Challenge:

You are happy where you live but circumstances have suddenly changed and you are told you have to move.

What response could you choose?
Happy/Unhappy

Results from **Everything Makes Me Happy Exercise**:

Make a note of everything through your day that makes you happy. Be specific.

Step 7

Write down anything further you want to do to increase your happiness.